This Journal Belongs To

© 2019 DeeRi Designs

All Rights Reserved

Book Layout, Illustration © DeeRi Designs

No part of this book may be reproduced, scanned or distributed in any printed or electronic form without prior permission from the author.

Word of the day	

Synonyms	Antonyms

Illustrate	Definition

Sentence	

Parts of speech	Number of vowels	Number of syllables

Word of the day	

Synonyms	Antonyms

Illustrate	Definition

Sentence		

Parts of speech	Number of vowels	Number of syllables

Word of the day	

Synonyms	Antonyms

Illustrate	Definition

Sentence

Parts of speech	Number of vowels	Number of syllables

Word of the day	

Synonyms	Antonyms

Illustrate	Definition

Sentence

Parts of speech	Number of vowels	Number of syllables

Word of the day	

Synonyms	Antonyms

Illustrate	Definition

Sentence

Parts of speech	Number of vowels	Number of syllables

Word of the day	

Synonyms	Antonyms

Illustrate	Definition

Sentence

Parts of speech	Number of vowels	Number of syllables

Word of the day	

Synonyms	Antonyms

Illustrate	Definition

Sentence	

Parts of speech	Number of vowels	Number of syllables

Word of the day	

Synonyms	Antonyms

Illustrate	Definition

Sentence

Parts of speech	Number of vowels	Number of syllables

Word of the day	

Synonyms	Antonyms

Illustrate	Definition

Sentence	

Parts of speech	Number of vowels	Number of syllables

Word of the day	

Synonyms	Antonyms

Illustrate	Definition

Sentence	

Parts of speech	Number of vowels	Number of syllables

Word of the day

Synonyms	Antonyms

Illustrate	Definition

Sentence

Parts of speech	Number of vowels	Number of syllables

Word of the day	

Synonyms	Antonyms

Illustrate	Definition

Sentence	

Parts of speech	Number of vowels	Number of syllables

Word of the day	

Synonyms	Antonyms

Illustrate	Definition

Sentence

Parts of speech	Number of vowels	Number of syllables

Word of the day

Synonyms

Antonyms

Illustrate

Definition

Sentence

Parts of speech	Number of vowels	Number of syllables

Word of the day	

Synonyms	Antonyms

Illustrate	Definition

Sentence

Parts of speech	Number of vowels	Number of syllables

Word of the day

Synonyms	Antonyms

Illustrate	Definition

Sentence

Parts of speech	Number of vowels	Number of syllables

Word of the day	

Synonyms	Antonyms

Illustrate	Definition

Sentence	

Parts of speech	Number of vowels	Number of syllables

Word of the day	

Synonyms	Antonyms

Illustrate	Definition

Sentence	

Parts of speech	Number of vowels	Number of syllables

Word of the day	

Synonyms	Antonyms

Illustrate	Definition

Sentence

Parts of speech	Number of vowels	Number of syllables

Word of the day

Synonyms	Antonyms

Illustrate	Definition

Sentence

Parts of speech	Number of vowels	Number of syllables

Word of the day	

Synonyms	Antonyms

Illustrate	Definition

Sentence		

Parts of speech	Number of vowels	Number of syllables

Word of the day	

Synonyms	Antonyms

Illustrate	Definition

Sentence

Parts of speech	Number of vowels	Number of syllables

Word of the day

| Synonyms | Antonyms |

Illustrate

Definition

Sentence

Parts of speech	Number of vowels	Number of syllables

Word of the day	

Synonyms	Antonyms

Illustrate	Definition

Sentence

Parts of speech	Number of vowels	Number of syllables

Word of the day	

Synonyms	Antonyms

Illustrate	Definition

Sentence

Parts of speech	Number of vowels	Number of syllables

Word of the day

Synonyms

Antonyms

Illustrate

Definition

Sentence

Parts of speech	Number of vowels	Number of syllables

Word of the day

Synonyms

Antonyms

Illustrate

Definition

Sentence

Parts of speech	Number of vowels	Number of syllables

Word of the day	

Synonyms	Antonyms

Illustrate	Definition

Sentence

Parts of speech	Number of vowels	Number of syllables

Word of the day	

Synonyms	Antonyms

Illustrate	Definition

Sentence

Parts of speech	Number of vowels	Number of syllables

Word of the day	

Synonyms	Antonyms

Illustrate	Definition

Sentence

Parts of speech	Number of vowels	Number of syllables

Word of the day

Synonyms	Antonyms

Illustrate	Definition

Sentence

Parts of speech	Number of vowels	Number of syllables

Word of the day

Synonyms

Antonyms

Illustrate

Definition

Sentence

Parts of speech	Number of vowels	Number of syllables

Word of the day	

Synonyms	Antonyms

Illustrate	Definition

Sentence

Parts of speech	Number of vowels	Number of syllables

Word of the day	

Synonyms	Antonyms

Illustrate	Definition

Sentence

Parts of speech	Number of vowels	Number of syllables

Word of the day

| Synonyms | Antonyms |

| Illustrate | Definition |

Sentence

Parts of speech	Number of vowels	Number of syllables

Word of the day	

Synonyms	Antonyms

Illustrate	Definition

Sentence

Parts of speech	Number of vowels	Number of syllables

Word of the day	

Synonyms	Antonyms

Illustrate	Definition

Sentence

Parts of speech	Number of vowels	Number of syllables

Word of the day	

Synonyms	Antonyms

Illustrate	Definition

Sentence

Parts of speech	Number of vowels	Number of syllables

Word of the day

Synonyms

Antonyms

Illustrate

Definition

Sentence

Parts of speech	Number of vowels	Number of syllables

Word of the day	

Synonyms	Antonyms

Illustrate	Definition

Sentence	

Parts of speech	Number of vowels	Number of syllables

Word of the day	

Synonyms	Antonyms

Illustrate	Definition

Sentence

Parts of speech	Number of vowels	Number of syllables

Word of the day

Synonyms	Antonyms

Illustrate	Definition

Sentence

Parts of speech	Number of vowels	Number of syllables

Word of the day	

Synonyms	Antonyms

Illustrate	Definition

Sentence

Parts of speech	Number of vowels	Number of syllables

Word of the day

Synonyms	Antonyms

Illustrate	Definition

Sentence

Parts of speech	Number of vowels	Number of syllables

Word of the day	

Synonyms	Antonyms

Illustrate	Definition

Sentence

Parts of speech	Number of vowels	Number of syllables

Word of the day	

Synonyms	Antonyms

Illustrate	Definition

Sentence	

Parts of speech	Number of vowels	Number of syllables

Word of the day	

Synonyms	Antonyms

Illustrate	Definition

Sentence

Parts of speech	Number of vowels	Number of syllables

Word of the day	

Synonyms	Antonyms

Illustrate	Definition

Sentence	

Parts of speech	Number of vowels	Number of syllables

Word of the day	

Synonyms	Antonyms

Illustrate	Definition

Sentence

Parts of speech	Number of vowels	Number of syllables

Word of the day

Synonyms	Antonyms

Illustrate	Definition

Sentence

Parts of speech	Number of vowels	Number of syllables

Word of the day	

Synonyms	Antonyms

Illustrate	Definition

Sentence

Parts of speech	Number of vowels	Number of syllables

Word of the day	

Synonyms	Antonyms

Illustrate	Definition

Sentence

Parts of speech	Number of vowels	Number of syllables

Word of the day

Synonyms

Antonyms

Illustrate

Definition

Sentence

Parts of speech	Number of vowels	Number of syllables

Word of the day

Synonyms	Antonyms

Illustrate	Definition

Sentence

Parts of speech	Number of vowels	Number of syllables

Word of the day	

Synonyms	Antonyms

Illustrate	Definition

Sentence

Parts of speech	Number of vowels	Number of syllables

Word of the day	

Synonyms	Antonyms

Illustrate	Definition

Sentence

Parts of speech	Number of vowels	Number of syllables

Word of the day

Synonyms	Antonyms

Illustrate	Definition

Sentence

Parts of speech	Number of vowels	Number of syllables

Word of the day	

Synonyms	Antonyms

Illustrate	Definition

Sentence

Parts of speech	Number of vowels	Number of syllables

Word of the day	
Synonyms	Antonyms
Illustrate	Definition
Sentence	

Parts of speech	Number of vowels	Number of syllables

Word of the day	

Synonyms	Antonyms

Illustrate	Definition

Sentence

Parts of speech	Number of vowels	Number of syllables

Word of the day	
Synonyms	Antonyms
Illustrate	Definition
Sentence	

Parts of speech	Number of vowels	Number of syllables

Word of the day	

Synonyms	Antonyms

Illustrate	Definition

Sentence	

Parts of speech	Number of vowels	Number of syllables

Word of the day	

Synonyms	Antonyms

Illustrate	Definition

Sentence

Parts of speech	Number of vowels	Number of syllables

Word of the day

Synonyms	Antonyms

Illustrate	Definition

Sentence

Parts of speech	Number of vowels	Number of syllables

Word of the day	

Synonyms	Antonyms

Illustrate	Definition

Sentence

Parts of speech	Number of vowels	Number of syllables

Word of the day	

Synonyms	Antonyms

Illustrate	Definition

Sentence

Parts of speech	Number of vowels	Number of syllables

Word of the day	

Synonyms	Antonyms

Illustrate	Definition

Sentence

Parts of speech	Number of vowels	Number of syllables

Word of the day	
Synonyms	Antonyms
Illustrate	Definition
Sentence	

Parts of speech	Number of vowels	Number of syllables

Word of the day	

Synonyms	Antonyms

Illustrate	Definition

Sentence

Parts of speech	Number of vowels	Number of syllables

Word of the day	

Synonyms	Antonyms

Illustrate	Definition

Sentence

Parts of speech	Number of vowels	Number of syllables

Word of the day	
Synonyms	**Antonyms**
Illustrate	**Definition**
Sentence	

Parts of speech	Number of vowels	Number of syllables

Word of the day	

Synonyms	Antonyms

Illustrate	Definition

Sentence

Parts of speech	Number of vowels	Number of syllables

Word of the day

Synonyms	Antonyms

Illustrate	Definition

Sentence

Parts of speech	Number of vowels	Number of syllables

Word of the day	

Synonyms	Antonyms

Illustrate	Definition

Sentence

Parts of speech	Number of vowels	Number of syllables

Word of the day	

Synonyms	Antonyms

Illustrate	Definition

Sentence

Parts of speech	Number of vowels	Number of syllables

Made in United States
Troutdale, OR
11/15/2023

14594385R00044